"HOW TO CODE: A PRACTICAL STEP-BY-STEP GUIDE FOR BEGINNERS

Contents

Prologue to Coding for Fledglings: Opening the Universe of Conceivable outcomes 3

1. Figuring out the Substance of Coding: 4

2. Setting Up Your Improvement Climate: 4

3. Leaving on Your Coding Process: 5

4. Opening the Force of Capabilities: 6

5. Exploring the Scene of Information Designs: 7

6. Embracing Article Arranged Programming (OOP): 7

1.1 What is Coding? 9

1.2 Why Take Coding Classes? 11

1.3 Arranging Your Improvement 14

2.1 Grasping Programming Dialects.................15

2.2 Picking Your Most memorable Programming Language 18

2.3 Composing Your First "Hi World" Program 20

3.1 Factors and Information Types 21

3.2 Administrators 24

3.3 Control Stream (if proclamations, circles) .26

4.1 Capacities for Portraying and Calling 29

Capacity with Limitations:............................30

4.2 Limits and Capacity to Restore Values
Capacity to Restore Values 30

4.3 Fixing Code into Modules 31

5.1 Clusters and Records..................................35

5.2 Word references (Cooperative Exhibits)....36

5.3 Strings 37

6.1 Classes and Items.......................................40

6.2 Legacy and Polymorphism 42

6.3 Exemplification and Deliberation...............45

7.1 Normal Blunders 48

Linguistic structure Blunders: 48

Rationale Blunders:.......................................49

7.2 Troubleshooting Methods 50

Print Proclamations: 50

Logging...50

7.3 Utilizing Troubleshooting Instruments 53

Incorporated Advancement Climate (IDE) Debuggers:...53

Pdb (Python Debugger):..............................53

Visual Studio Code Debugger:.......................54

8.1 Prologue to Git...55

Adaptation Control: 55

Basic Ideas: 55

8.2 Essential Git Orders.....................................57

Introducing a Vault: 57

Arranging Changes:.....................................57

Committing Changes:...................................57

8.3 Working together on Activities with Git 59

Cloning a Store:...59

Making a Branch: 60

9.1 Simple Projects for Beginners Daily agenda Application:..62

9.2 Project Walkthroughs, Step-by-Step Plan for the day Application:..64

Step 1: Establish the structure of the project (HTML, CSS, and JavaScript files). 64

2. Straightforward Page: 65

3. Calculator:...65

4. Climate Application:...................................66

5. Talk Application: 66

6. Individual Portfolio Site:...........................67

Conclusion...69

Prologue to Coding for Fledglings: Opening the Universe of Conceivable outcomes

In the quickly developing scene of innovation, coding has turned into a fundamental expertise that opens ways to a bunch of chances. Whether you are keen on making sites, creating versatile applications, investigating information, or in any event, jumping into the domains of man-made brainpower, figuring out how to code gives you the devices to rejuvenate your thoughts. This beginner's guide to coding is intended to serve as your compass on this exciting journey by providing a structured path to understanding the fundamentals of programming and beginning a rewarding adventure in the field.

1. Figuring out the Substance of Coding:

The first step is to dispel the myths surrounding coding. What precisely is coding, and for what reason is it applicable in the present advanced age? We'll investigate the primary standards behind coding, separating complex specialized language into effectively absorbable pieces. By the time you get to the end of this section, you will not only know how important coding is but also how much it affects a lot of different industries.

2. Setting Up Your Improvement Climate:

Exploring the immense scene of coding can be overpowering, however dread not! We'll direct you through the method involved with setting up your improvement climate. This section ensures that you are well-prepared to begin writing your first lines of code. It covers everything from selecting a programming language to installing essential tools.

3. Leaving on Your Coding Process:

With the nuts and bolts set up, now is the right time to plunge into the universe of programming. We'll acquaint you with the central ideas that structure the structure blocks of coding. Points, for example, factors, information types, and control stream will turn out to be natural as you leave on active activities that harden your comprehension.

4. Opening the Force of Capabilities:

As your coding ability develops, you'll find the significance of putting together code into reusable units called capabilities. This segment dives into the craft of characterizing, calling, and upgrading capabilities, engaging you to compose more effective and particular code.

5. Exploring the Scene of Information Designs:

Data structures are a prerequisite for any coding course. We'll investigate the universe of exhibits, records, word references, and strings, giving you the apparatuses to really control and oversee information. Any effective software program is built on these fundamental abilities.

6. Embracing Article Arranged Programming (OOP):

Object-situated writing computer programs is a worldview that permits you to display true elements in your code. In this part, you'll gain proficiency with the standards of OOP, including classes, items, legacy, and embodiment. This information will hoist your abilities to code, empowering you to configuration more refined and viable programming.

As you progress through this aide, you'll acquire specialized capability as well as develop critical thinking abilities and an imaginative mentality. Coding isn't just about composing lines of text; it's tied in with making arrangements, releasing advancement, and adding to the always growing computerized scene. Thus, we should set out on this excursion together, disentangling the secrets of coding and opening a universe of conceivable outcomes readily available. Prepare to code your fantasies into the real world!

1.1 What is Coding?

The method involved with composing a bunch of guidelines that advise a PC how to complete an undertaking is known as coding, or programming. These rules are written in a programming language, a coordinated and purposeful game plan of concludes that computers can grasp and execute. Coding is, at its core, a means of communicating with machines and people. It engages us to create a translation of our viewpoints into a language that laptops can interpret and circle back to.

In coding, we use express sentence construction and orders to make computations and tasks. An estimation is a one small step at a time system or recipe for dealing with an issue, while a program is a lot of rules that, when executed, plays out a particular endeavor or handles a specific issue. Whether it's arranging a site, making a versatile application, or looking at data, coding is the best approach to changing thoughts into utilitarian, executable game plans.

Learning to code opens up a world of possibilities, allowing people to create programming, automate tasks, and advance in a variety of fields. It is the underpinning of development and the fundamental catalyst behind the high level change framing our state of the art world.

1.2 Why Take Coding Classes?

Coding isn't only for programmers or PC researchers; it is a critical skill for individuals in various reasons for living. Here are persuading inspirations to set out on the journey of getting coding:

a. Decisive Abilities to reason:

Your ability to reason eloquently and critically is challenged by coding. It urges you to isolate complex issues into reasonable parts and devise purposeful plans.

b. Possibilities for Business:

In today's technology-driven society, coding skills are in high demand across all industries. Capacity in coding clears the path for a wide bunch of livelihood open entryways, from programming improvement and data assessment to organize security and mechanized thinking.

c. Innovativeness and Progression:
Coding is an imaginative procedure that grants you to restore your contemplations. It empowers you to build applications, locales, and automated courses of action, empowering headway and ambitious endeavors.

d. Sorting out Development:
Coding gives understanding into how development capabilities. It furnishes you with a more profound cognizance of the computerized world by demystifying the product and frameworks we use consistently.

e. Future-Fixing Your Capacities:

As development continues to drive, coding instruction ends up being dynamically critical. Learning to code equips you with useful skills that can help you adapt to the shifting demands of the job market.

1.3 Arranging Your Improvement

Climate Before You Start Coding It's Critical to Design Your Advancement Climate This incorporates setting up your PC with the crucial contraptions and programming to make, test, and run your code capably. The means for setting up an improvement environment could contrast depending upon your picked programming language and stage. In the impending fragments, we'll guide you through the cycle, ensuring that you have a steady and helpful coding experience. Accordingly, we should put on our coding caps and prepare to enter the intriguing scene!

2.1 Grasping Programming Dialects

Programming dialects act as a vehicle for correspondence among people and PCs. They permit us to pass directions on to machines in a manner that is organized, sensible, and justifiable. There are various programming dialects, each with its own grammar, rules, and use cases. To help you comprehend programming languages, here are some fundamental ideas:

a. Punctuation:

Grammar alludes to the arrangement of decides that direct the way in which projects written in a specific language ought to be organized. It incorporates shows for composing articulations, proclaiming factors, and characterizing capabilities.

Sentence structure blunders happen when these standards are not kept accurately.

b. Languages at different levels:
High-level languages like Python and JavaScript are made to be easy for humans to read and write. Conversely, low-level dialects, like Get together, give more straightforward command over equipment yet are less lucid.

c. Assembled versus Deciphered Dialects:
A few dialects are ordered, meaning the code is converted into machine code before execution (e.g., C++). Others are deciphered, where the code is executed line by line by a mediator (e.g., Python). There are benefits and drawbacks to each strategy.

d. Application Areas:

Programming dialects are frequently customized to explicit application spaces. For instance, web improvement frequently includes dialects like HTML, CSS, and JavaScript, while information science might utilize dialects like Python and R.

Understanding these central ideas will assist you with exploring the assorted scene of programming dialects and settle on informed conclusions about which language to learn in light of your objectives and interests.

2.2 Picking Your Most memorable Programming Language

Picking the right programming language for your initial steps is a pivotal choice. Every language has its assets, and the decision relies upon elements, for example, your objectives, the kind of tasks you need to chip away at, and the assets accessible. Here are a few famous dialects for novices:

a. Python:

Known for its clarity and effortlessness, Python is an incredible decision for amateurs. It has a tremendous local area and is broadly utilized in web improvement, information science, and computerized reasoning.

b. JavaScript:

Fundamental for web advancement, JavaScript permits you to make dynamic and intuitive sites. A flexible language can likewise be utilized for server-side turn of events (Node.js).

c. Java:

Java is a flexible language known for its "compose once, run anyplace" theory. It is utilized in a wide range of applications, including enterprise-level systems and mobile development (Android).

d. Scratch:

In the event that you're totally new to coding, Scratch is a visual programming language intended for fledglings. It utilizes a simplified connection point, making it open for kids and grown-ups the same.

2.3 Composing Your First "Hi World" Program

The "Hi World" program is a basic yet conventional method for starting off your coding process. It entails creating a program that sends the message "Hello, World!" to the user. to the display. This starting activity assists you with figuring out the fundamental construction of a program and guarantees that your improvement climate is set up accurately.

We should investigate a straightforward "Hi World" program in Python:

```python
Duplicate code
# Python Hi World Program
print("Hello, World!")
```

This compact program utilizes the print capability to show the predefined text. As you progress in your coding experience, you'll expand upon this establishment, step by step adding intricacy and usefulness to your projects.

Now that you grasp programming dialects, have picked a language to begin with, and composed your most memorable program, you're prepared to dive further into the interesting universe of coding. In the impending segments, we'll investigate crucial ideas and guide you through active activities to build up your comprehension. Have fun coding!

3.1 Factors and Information Types

Factors:

In programming, factors are utilized to store and oversee information. Consider them compartments that hold data. Every variable has a name and a worth. For instance, in Python:

```python
Duplicate code
# Variable model
age = 25
name = "John"
```

Here, age and name are factors. age is represented by an integer, while name is represented by a string (text). Picking significant variable names makes your code more intelligible and reasonable.

Information Types:
The kinds of data that a variable can hold are known as data types. Some common types of data are:

Number (int): Entire numbers without decimals (e.g., 5, - 2).

Float (float): Numbers with decimals (e.g., 3.14, - 0.5).

String (str): Text encased in statements (e.g., "Hi, World!").

(bool) Boolean: Addresses either Evident or Misleading.

python

Duplicate code

```python
# Information type models
integer_number = 42
float_number = 3.14
text = "Hi, World!"
is_valid = Valid
```

Understanding factors and information types is crucial to controlling and handling data in your projects.

3.2 Administrators

Administrators are images that perform procedure on factors and values. There are different kinds of administrators:

Number-crunching Administrators: Perform numerical tasks.

```python
Duplicate code
expansion = 5 + 3
deduction = 10 - 4
augmentation = 2 * 6
division = 8/2
```

Examination Administrators: Look at values and return a Boolean outcome.

```python
Duplicate code
is_equal = (5 == 5) # Valid
is_not_equal = (7 ! = 3) # Valid
```

Intelligent Administrators: Join Boolean qualities.

Python's copy code has the following assignment operators: logical_and = True or False # False # True Allot values to factors.

python
Duplicate code
x = 10
x += 5 # Comparable to x = x + 5
Understanding how to utilize administrators permits you to play out a great many tasks in your projects.

3.3 Control Stream (if proclamations, circles)

If Articulations:

Contingent articulations, frequently utilized with the if catchphrase, permit you to execute different code blocks in light of conditions.

```python
Duplicate code
# If proclamation model
age = 18
if age >= 18:
    "You are an adult." print
else:
    print("You are a minor.")
```

Here, the program checks assuming age is more prominent than or equivalent to 18 and executes the comparing block of code.

Loops:

Circles empower you to rehash a block of code on different occasions.

a. While Circle:

Python Copy Code # While Loop Example: count = 0 while count is greater than 5:

```
    print("Count:", count)
    count += 1
```

This circle prints the worth of count until it arrives at 5.

b. For Circle:

Python Copy code # An example of a for loop for i in a range(3):

```
    print("Iteration:", I)
```

This circle emphasizes multiple times, with I taking qualities 0, 1, and 2.

For creating programs that are both responsive and dynamic, control flow structures like if statements and loops are essential. They empower you to make code that adjusts to various circumstances and cycles information all the more productively. As you proceed with your coding process, these ideas will turn into the structure blocks for additional mind boggling and modern projects.

4.1 Capacities for Portraying and Calling

Abilities are fundamental for breaking code into estimated and reusable parts. They have a lot of rules, so you can call and use them on a variety of occasions usually through your program. This is how you depict and call limits:

Depicting Limits:
python
Duplicate code

```python
# Capacity definition
def welcome():
    print("Hello, there!")
```

\# In this model, the capacity welcome is a capacity that prints a welcome. # Calling welcome() The ability's code is executed when welcome() is called.

Capacity with Limitations:

Capabilities have access to outside information for management thanks to their capacity to recognize boundaries.

Python code copy # Capacity with limits def greet_person(name):

```
    print("Hello, " + name + "!")
```

Calling the limit with a contention greet_person("Alice")
Here, greet_person takes a cutoff name, and when the limit is called with a contention ("Alice"), it prints a changed welcoming.

4.2 Limits and Capacity to Restore Values Capacity to Restore Values

Functions can also return values, giving the code that is calling them a way to get information.

Python Copy Code # Ability to Reestablish Worth Definition add_numbers(a, b):

```
    # Summoning the capacity and putting the result sum_result = add_numbers(3, 5) print("Sum:", sum_result)
```

In this model, add_numbers adds two limits (an and b), returns the outcome, and afterward does likewise for the other limit. The returned respect is then dealt with in sum_result and printed.

4.3 Fixing Code into Modules

As your codebase makes, sorting out it becomes crucial for possibility. Modules permit you to part your code into discrete records, each containing related capacities and factors. A straightforward layout is according to the accompanying:

Module: math_operations.py
python
Duplicate code

```python
# math_operations.py
def add(a, b):
    return a + b

def subtract(a, b):
    return a - b
```

Boss Program: main_program.py
python
Duplicate code

```python
# main_program.py
import math_operations

result_add = math_operations.add(10, 5)
result_subtract = math_operations.subtract(10, 5)
```

```
print("Addition                Result:",
result_add)
print("Subtraction             Result:",
result_subtract)
```

Math_operations.py capabilities as a module in this model, giving extension and derivation capacities. The main_program.py record imports and uses these capacities, keeping the code made and isolated.

Forming code that is flexible and easy to stay aware of requires an understanding of capacities and modularization. By isolating them into additional unobtrusive, more sensible parts, it makes it possible to make astounding structures. Modularization is especially valuable in agreeable endeavors and keeping in mind that overseeing tremendous codebases as you progress through your coding cycle.

5.1 Clusters and Records

Clusters:

A cluster is an information structure that stores an assortment of components, each recognized by a record or a key. In some programming dialects, clusters have a proper size, while in others, similar to Python, they can powerfully resize.

python
Duplicate code
# Cluster model in Python
numbers = [1, 2, 3, 4, 5]
print(numbers[2]) # Getting to the component at list 2 (yield: 3)

Lists:

In contrast to arrays, list elements can be of a variety of data types and are more adaptable in size. In Python, records are a flexible and broadly utilized information structure.

python
Duplicate code
List model in Python
organic products = ["apple", "banana", "orange"]
print(fruits[1]) # Getting to the component at file 1 (yield: banana)
Effectively organizing and manipulating data collections in your programs requires an understanding of arrays and lists.

5.2 Word references (Cooperative Exhibits)

Word references, otherwise called cooperative exhibits or guides, are information structures that store key-esteem matches. Each key in a word reference guides to a particular worth, permitting you to rapidly recover values.

python
Duplicate code

```python
# Word reference model in Python
individual = {"name": " Alice", "age": 25, "city": " Wonderland"}
print(person["age"]) # Getting to
```

the worth related with the key "age" (yield: 25) When you need to show how various pieces of information relate to one another, dictionaries come in handy.

5.3 Strings

Strings are arrangements of characters and are perhaps of the most well-known datum types in programming. They permit you to work with text and are frequently utilized for information, result, and control.

```python
Duplicate code
# String models in Python
message = "Hi, World!"
print(len(message)) # Length of the string (yield: 13) # String concatenation greeting = "Hello" name = "Alice" full_greeting = greeting + ", " + name + "!"
print(full_greeting) # Result: Hi, Alice!
```

You'll be able to handle and process a wide range of data in your programs if you know how to use arrays, lists, strings, and dictionaries. These information structures are the structure blocks for making complex applications and calculations. As you proceed to investigate and dominate them, you'll acquire the capacity to proficiently settle many computational issues.

6.1 Classes and Items

Classes:

In object-situated programming (OOP), a class is an outline or layout for making objects. It characterizes a bunch of qualities and ways of behaving that the articles made from the class will have.

python
Duplicate code

```python
# Class model in Python
class Canine:
    def _init_(self, name, age):
        self.name = name
        self.age = age

    def bark(self):
        print("Woof!")

# Making an article (occasion) of
the Canine class
```

```python
my_dog = Dog(name="Buddy", age=3)
```

Objects:

Objects are examples of a class. They address explicit elements with extraordinary traits and ways of behaving characterized by the class.

python
Duplicate code

```python
# Getting to credits and summoning strategies for an article
print(my_dog.name) # Result: Mate
my_dog.bark() # Result: Woof!
```

Understanding classes and items permits you to demonstrate and address genuine elements in your projects.

6.2 Legacy and Polymorphism

Legacy:

Legacy is an instrument that permits another class (subclass or determined class) to acquire qualities and ways of behaving from a current class (base class or superclass).

python
Duplicate code

```python
# Legacy model in Python
class Vehicle:
    def __init__(self, brand):
        self.brand = brand

    def start_engine(self):
        print("Engine began.")

# Subclass acquiring from the Vehicle class
class ElectricCar(Car):
    def charge_battery(self):
```

```python
    print("Battery charging.")

# Making objects of the two classes
my_car = Car(brand="Toyota")
my_electric_car              = ElectricCar(brand="Tesla")

# Utilizing acquired strategies
my_car.start_engine()   #   Result: Motor turned over.
my_electric_car.charge_battery()   # Result: Battery charging.
```

Polymorphism:

Polymorphism permits objects of various classes to be treated as objects of a typical base class. It advances code adaptability and reusability.

python
Duplicate code

```python
# Polymorphism model in Python
def introduce_vehicle(vehicle):
```

```
    print(f"I own a {vehicle.brand}.")
```

```
# Utilizing polymorphism with
objects of various classes
introduce_vehicle(my_car) # Result:
Toyota is my car.
#                         Output:
introduce_vehicle(my_electric_car).
I own a Tesla.
```

Legacy and polymorphism empower you to make various leveled and reusable code structures.

6.3 Exemplification and Deliberation

Exemplification:

Exemplification includes packaging information (properties) and techniques that work on that information into a solitary unit, known as a class. It helps keep the inside workings of a class hidden from the outside world.

Python copy code # Encapsulation example for the BankAccount class in Python:

```python
    def __init__(self, balance):
        self._balance = balance  # Embodiment utilizing a confidential characteristic

    def get_balance(self):
        bring self._balance back

    def deposit(self, sum):
```

```python
        self._balance += sum

    def withdraw(self, sum):
        if sum <= self._balance:
            self._balance - = sum
        else:
            print("Insufficient reserves.")
```

Abstraction:

Reflection includes improving on complex frameworks by demonstrating classes in light of fundamental properties and ways of behaving. It permits you to zero in on the applicable parts of an article and overlook the superfluous subtleties.

python
Duplicate code
```python
# Deliberation model in Python
class Shape:
    def calculate_area(self):
```

```
    raise
NotImplementedError("Subclasses
should carry out this strategy.")

# Subclass giving a substantial
execution
class Circle(Shape):
  def __init__(self, range):
    self.radius = range

  def calculate_area(self):
    return 3.14 * self.radius ** 2
```
Epitome and deliberation work with code association, support, and the formation of secluded, reasonable frameworks. They are key standards in planning powerful and versatile article situated programs.

7.1 Normal Blunders
Linguistic structure Blunders:

Punctuation blunders happen when the code abuses the writing computer programs language's guidelines, making it unfit to be deciphered or incorporated.

python
Duplicate code

```
# Sentence structure mistake model
print("Hello, World"
```

Runtime Blunders:

Runtime blunders happen during the execution of a program and commonly result from surprising circumstances or invalid tasks.

python
Duplicate code

```
# Runtime blunder model (ZeroDivisionError)
result = 10/0
```

Rationale Blunders:

Rationale mistakes don't make the program crash however bring about wrong way of behaving. These blunders frequently come from botches in the program's calculation or rationale.

python
Duplicate code
```
# Rationale blunder model
def calculate_area(radius):
    return 2 * 3.14 * sweep # Wrong
recipe
```
Understanding normal blunders is fundamental for viable investigating and investigating.

7.2 Troubleshooting Methods

Print Proclamations:

Adding print proclamations to your code permits you to assess the upsides of factors at various places in the program, distinguishing issues.

python
Duplicate code

```python
# Involving print articulations for troubleshooting
def calculate_area(radius):
    print("Debugging:", sweep)
    return 3.14 * sweep ** 2
```

Logging:

Logging gives a more deliberate method for following the progression of your program. You can utilize the logging module to yield messages at various seriousness levels.

54

```python
Duplicate code
# Involving logging for investigating
import logging

def calculate_area(radius):
    "Debugging: %" in logging.debug
s", range)
    return 3.14 * sweep ** 2
```

Special case Dealing with:

Enclose possibly mistake inclined code by attempt with the exception of blocks to effortlessly deal with blunders and forestall program crashes.

```python
Duplicate code
# Exemption dealing with for investigating
def safe_divide(a, b):
    try:
```

result = a / b return the result with the exception of ZeroDivisionError:

print("Error: Division by nothing.")

bring None back

7.3 Utilizing Troubleshooting Instruments

Incorporated Advancement Climate (IDE) Debuggers:

Current IDEs come furnished with investigating devices that permit you to set breakpoints, examine factors, and step through your code line by line.

Pdb (Python Debugger):

The underlying pdb module gives a debugger to Python. You can embed breakpoints in your code and run it in intelligent mode.

```python
Duplicate code
# Utilizing pdb for troubleshooting
import pdb

def calculate_area(radius):
```

```
pdb.set_trace()  # Embedding a
breakpoint
    return 3.14 * sweep ** 2
```

Visual Studio Code Debugger:

On the off chance that you're utilizing Visual Studio Code, it offers a strong debugger with highlights like variable investigation, breakpoints, and step-through execution.

Dominating troubleshooting methods and apparatuses is critical for recognizing and fixing issues in your code effectively. These skills will help you create programs that are both robust and error-free, whether you use print statements, logging, or advanced debugging tools.

8.1 Prologue to Git

Adaptation Control:

Form control is a framework that permits you to follow changes in your codebase after some time. It empowers coordinated effort, works with rollback to past states, and gives a background marked by changes.

Git:

Git is a circulated rendition control framework generally utilized in programming improvement. It permits different designers to chip away at a venture at the same time while keeping a total history of changes.

Basic Ideas:

Store (Repo): An assortment of documents and their modification history.

Commit: A preview of changes made to the code at a particular moment.

Branch: a code version that is independent of the main development path.

8.2 Essential Git Orders

Introducing a Vault:

To begin involving Git in your undertaking, explore to your venture's root registry and run:

Changes are staged and committed using bash and git init.

Arranging Changes:

slam
Duplicate code
git add filename # Stage a particular record
git add .   # Stage all changes

Committing Changes:

slam
Duplicate code
git commit - m "Commit message"

Actually looking at Archive Status:

To see the situation with your storehouse and arranged changes:

slam
Duplicate code
git status
Seeing Commit History:
To see the commit history:

slam
Duplicate code
git log

8.3 Working together on Activities with Git

Cloning a Store:

To make a nearby duplicate of a far off vault:

slam
Duplicate code
git clone remote_url
Pushing Changes to a Distant Storehouse:

To push your nearby changes to a far off store:

slam
Duplicate code
git push beginning branch_name
Pulling Changes from a Distant Storehouse:

To get changes from a distant vault and consolidation them into your neighborhood office:

Branching and merging: bash Copy code git pull origin branch_name
Making a Branch:

bash Copy code to the git branch with the name branch_name # Create a new branch Switching Branches:

slam
Duplicate code
git checkout branch_name # Change to a current branch
Combining Branches:

slam
Duplicate code
git combine branch_name # Consolidation changes from a branch into the ongoing branch
Understanding these fundamental Git orders is fundamental for dealing with your task's variant

history and teaming up actually with others. Whether you're dealing with a performance project or adding to a collaboration, Git's strong elements smooth out the improvement interaction and assist with keeping away from clashes.

9.1 Simple Projects for Beginners
Daily agenda Application:

Make an easy plan for the day application where clients can add, erase, and mark undertakings as finished. This venture will include working with client input, information capacity, and fundamental UI components.

2. Straightforward Website page:

Fabricate a fundamental individual site page utilizing HTML and CSS. Incorporate areas like a presentation, abilities, and contact data. This venture is perfect for getting involved insight with web advancement.

3. Calculator:

Foster a number cruncher application that can perform fundamental math tasks. This undertaking will assist you with rehearsing client input taking care of and essential numerical rationale.

4. Climate Application:
Fabricate a straightforward climate application that brings and shows climate data in light of client input (city or postal division). Handling JSON data and working with APIs are part of this project.

5. Talk Application:
Utilize real-time messaging or a straightforward chatbot to create a basic chat application. This task will include working with client input, server-side programming (if utilizing constant informing), and taking care of messages.

6. Individual Portfolio Site:

Upgrade your web improvement abilities by making an individual portfolio site. Feature your activities, abilities, and contact data. This venture will include HTML, CSS, and potentially JavaScript for intelligence.

9.2 Project Walkthroughs, Step-by-Step Plan for the day Application:

Step 1: Establish the structure of the project (HTML, CSS, and JavaScript files).

Step 2: Make the UI for adding, erasing, and stamping assignments.

Step 3: Put the logic in place to handle user input and keep the task list up to date.

Step 4: Make the application look good by styling it.

Step 5: Test the application to guarantee it functions true to form.

2. Straightforward Page:

Step 1: Plan the format of your site page utilizing HTML.

Step 2: Style your site page involving CSS for an outwardly engaging look.

Step 3: Add content like a presentation, abilities, and contact data.

Step 4: Test your site page on various programs to guarantee similarity.

3. Calculator:

Step 1: Set up the calculator's HTML structure.

Step 2: Style the mini-computer utilizing CSS.

Step 3: Execute the JavaScript rationale for performing fundamental number juggling activities.

Step 4: Test the mini-computer with different contributions to guarantee precise estimations.

4. Climate Application:

Step 1: Set up the HTML structure for the climate application.

Step 2: Style the application utilizing CSS.

Step 3: To obtain weather data based on user input, make use of a weather API.

Step 4: Show the recovered climate data on the application.

Step 5: Test the application with various areas to check precise climate information recovery.

5. Talk Application:

Step 1: Set up the task structure.

Step 2: Make a basic UI for sending and getting messages.

Step 3: Carry out the rationale for dealing with client messages.

Step 4: In the event that utilizing constant informing, set up a server to deal with informing usefulness.

Step 5: Test the application by sending and getting messages.

6. Individual Portfolio Site:

Step 1: Plan the format and construction of your portfolio utilizing HTML.

Step 2: Apply styling to your portfolio utilizing CSS.

Step 3: Add content, for example, project subtleties, abilities, and contact data.

Step 4: Consider adding intuitiveness involving JavaScript for a more unique encounter.

Step 5: Test your portfolio site on various gadgets to guarantee responsiveness.

These bit by bit walkthroughs give an organized way to deal with building basic tasks. They cover everything from basic HTML and CSS to working with APIs and JavaScript. As you complete these undertakings, you'll acquire functional experience and trust in your abilities to code.

Conclusion.

All things considered, passing on the trip of sorting out some way to code opens up a vast expanse of possible results and draws in you to restore your considerations. This fledgling's coding guide has spread out a way for you to follow as you become familiar with the crucial thoughts and abilities that each hopeful software engineer needs. From understanding the stray pieces of coding and setting up your improvement environment to exploring data structures, object-organized programming, and variation control with Git, you've obtained encounters into the middle parts of programming progression.

Participating in active tasks and applying the concepts you've learned to real-world situations is essential as you progress through the coding process. Building direct undertakings upholds your understanding as well as instills decisive abilities to reason and ingenuity. Each project helps you grow as a coder, whether you decide to create a plan for the day application, a personal portfolio site, or a visit application.

In addition, the associate familiar you with the basic capacities of exploring and dealing with botches, key for staying aware of code quality and researching issues, as a matter of fact. Besides, version control with Git was presented as a huge instrument for managing code changes, collaborating with others, and keeping a coordinated improvement process.

Keep in mind that coding is more than just writing lines of code; It is connected to solving problems, expressing imagination, and contributing to the ever-evolving computerized scene. As you continue with your coding cycle, stay curious, research new advances, and feel free to handle testing projects. Coding is a tremendous and consistently developing field that gives innumerable chances to learning and development.

Whether you want to code for personal projects, a specific career path, or just for the fun of it, the skills you've developed will provide a solid foundation. Keep coding, keep learning, and embrace the fascinating possibilities that lie ahead. Have a good time coding!

www.ingramcontent.com/pod-product-compliance
Lightning Source LLC
LaVergne TN
LVHW051608050326
832903LV00033B/4406